# Friends of the Earth
## Yearbook

# Introduction

Rachel Moreton

There have been many jokes about 'little green people' who live on other planets and visit Earth. If there are such alien beings (and it's rather doubtful!), they probably do a better job of looking after their planet than we do ours!

The fact is, us 'Earthlings' need to become green people ourselves. We're not just visiting Earth, we're staying, so we really need to look after our home. It's not a joke - there are some pretty worrying environmental problems - but helping the environment can and should be fun. If you want to be a green person, you need to know about the problems, and about what you can do to help. This book is a good place to start. Over to you...

# The Vanishing Forests

If you lived in a rainforest, from morning to night you would be aware of trees. You would see trees, smell trees and play among them. Some of your tribe would go hunting while others built houses or cooked meals. Just think what this would be like!

Look around (where you live) and see how many trees are growing. Unless you are very lucky there will probably only be a few. Trees have been cut down over thousands of years for many reasons. These include clearing land to grow crops and getting wood for building and fuel. But now it is tropical rainforests that are under threat.

Rainforests are found in tropical parts of the world, where the climate is hot and wet. These forests are very different from those in cooler places such as Britain or North America. (See map).

Tropical rainforests get at least 4 metres of rain every year - and some get as much as 10 metres. This is more than six times as much as the average rainfall we get in Britain. Sometimes the rain is so heavy that you can

Hans Rainhard / Tony Stone Worldwide
Tony Stone Worldwide

be soaked to the skin in seconds.

## Life in the forests

Rainforests are home to many strange and beautiful plants and animals. The world's largest flower, the unpleasant smelling Rafflesia Arnoldii, is found in the Sumatran rainforest, and is now becoming quite rare.

These forests contain more different types of plant and animal than anywhere else on Earth.

## Rainforest animals

Many types of animals are found in rainforests including: elephants, rhinoceroses, tigers, jaguars, monkeys and gorillas. The constant sound of insects and calls of

# Contents

©1990 Friends of the Earth

Written by Barbara James, John Howson and Steven Pollock.
Edited by Stephen Sterling and John Howson.
Editorial Assistant, Kesta Desmond. Layout and design by Louise Ivimy.

Acknowledgements: The authors would like to thank the following people and
organisations who helped with the book:
John Baines, ROSPA, the staff and volunteers of Friends of the Earth but particularly
Rupert Harwood, Athena Lamnisos, Neil Verlander and Adeela Warley.

Illustrations by Steve Weatherill, John Davey, Karen Hayles, Lesley McCubbin,
Dominic Parker and Robert Thompson.

Photographs supplied by and are copyright: Friends of the Earth, Tony Stone
Worldwide, Environmental Picture Library, Natural History Photographic Agency,
Animal Aid, Roger Hiorns, BTCV.

This book is printed on recycled paper.

Published by
**Grandreams Ltd,**
Jadwin House, 205 / 211 Kentish Town Road, London, NW5 2JU.

Printed in Belgium.

ISBN 0 86227 7930

animals fill the air day and night. Some of these animals eat plants, others hunt for meat, but all of the animals are perfectly adapted to life in the forest habitat.

Some animals are now in danger of becoming extinct, because the rainforests are disappearing. The golden lion tamarin of South America is one of the Earth's rarest animals, and was thought to be extinct, until a small colony was discovered. The orangutan, woolly spider monkey and scarlet macaw are all threatened.

Unfortunately, quite a few animals have already become extinct including the Javan tiger and many types of bird and butterfly. Sadly, in Colombia, over 500 types of bird have disappeared forever.

## Tribal peoples

Many different groups of peoples have lived in rainforests for thousands of years. The life of rainforest peoples fits in with the

Simon Counsell and Friends Of The Earth

forest; every part of their lives is based on the forest. Many hunt animals and farm small plots of land. After a few years the people move on and clear a new area of forest, leaving the old one to grow again.

The forest recovers easily from this type of farming because the plots are so small - something like the area that would be cleared naturally by a few trees falling in a storm.

Unless things change, the tribal peoples' culture and amazing knowledge of the forest and uses of plants will be lost forever.

*Above*: **A Penan family, now under threat in Sarawak.**

Nigel Dickenson / Environmental Picture Library

### The Penan

The Penan in Sarawak, Malaysia are one of the few remaining tribes that live by hunting and gathering. Forest in Sarawak is being cut down for timber.

Some tribes people decided to try to stop the loggers by forming human chains in front of logging roads. Over a hundred of these people were arrested and put in prison.

This is what one of the Penan said to try and stop the Sarawak Government allowing the forest to be cut down:

"Stop destroying the forest or we will be forced to protect it. The forest is our livelihood. We have lived here before any of you outsiders came. We fished in clean rivers and hunted in the jungle. We made our sago meat and ate fruit of the trees, our life was not easy but we lived content. Now the logging companies have turned the rivers into muddy streams and the jungle into devastation. The fish cannot survive in dirty rivers and wild animals will not live in devastated forest."

Herbert Girardet / Environmental Picture Library

## Forest destruction

The rainforests are rapidly being destroyed. This is happening for many reasons. Some countries with rainforests owe a lot of money to richer countries. For this reason these countries cut down their forest to sell the timber, and make room for more farms.

Farmers who have no land, clear areas of rainforest, usually by burning the trees. They use the land to grow crops, but the soil is not very fertile and so after a year or two they need to burn new areas again. So much land is being burned every year that the forest does not have a chance to recover. The land left behind is virtually useless, and is often used for cattle ranching although it is not good for this either.

Logging is another way in which the rainforest is destroyed. The wood is largely sold to richer western countries where it is used to make furniture and fittings. Logging is very destructive even where all the trees aren't removed.

Rainforest is also being destroyed through land being cleared for mines and large dams.

This destruction is contributing to the greenhouse effect. (See P.42).

Alex Olah / Environmental Picture Library

## Rainforest products

The next time that you are eating chocolate or drinking cola or chewing gum or eating crisps, think of the rainforests. All of these products use plants found in the forest as their main ingredient.

Tomatoes, potatoes, pineapples, maize or sweet corn, cocoa and rice were all first discovered in rainforests. Some people gather nuts, and remove latex for rubber, from trees in rainforests for a living. This does not harm the forest because no trees are removed.

Scenes of forest devastation caused by burning (*above left*) and logging (*above right and below*).

## Saving the forests

It will not be easy to save the forests.

Organisations such as Friends of the Earth are helping to prevent more forest being cut down. They are doing this by helping local people to protect the forest and by trying to convince governments to conserve them.

### Do something!

● Write and ask for details of the material published by Friends of the Earth about the rainforest.

● Try to convince adults not to buy products made from tropical hardwood.

The steaming jungle of the Amazon rainforest is home to thousands of rare plants and animals found nowhere else. Hiding in here, down and across, are 15 of the animals. CAN YOU FIND THEM?

Sloth Parrot Toucan Macaw
Anaconda Bat Monkey Peccary Tapir
Jaguar Hummingbird Boa River Dolphin Anteater Soldier Ant

| P | E | N | T | J | O | G | T | A | P | I | R |
| R | M | A | C | A | W | R | M | N | A | B | P |
| I | N | O | G | G | S | L | O | T | H | O | E |
| V | E | T | O | U | C | A | N | E | P | A | C |
| E | M | A | B | A | T | S | K | A | I | O | C |
| R | P | A | R | R | O | T | E | T | R | E | A |
| D | O | L | P | H | I | N | Y | E | A | K | R |
| A | N | A | C | O | N | D | A | R | N | O | Y |
| F | H | U | M | M | I | N | G | B | I | R | D |
| F | G | S | O | L | D | I | E | R | A | N | T |

start

CAN YOU FIND YOUR WAY THROUGH THE RAINFOREST, A

THE DANGERS, AND WITHOUT DISTURBING THE WILDLIFE?

# A PLACE IN THE FOREST

Here are 12 animals that live in the world's rainforests.
Can you place them in the picture?
Look for the outlines

ANACONDA
SNAKE

ARMADILLO

TAPIR

MORPHO
BUTTERFLY

TOUCAN

FLYING
SQUIRREL

TREE FROG

ORANG
UTAN

TIGER

LEOPARD

HUMMING
BIRD

BIRD EATING
SPIDER

Steve Weatherill 90

# Home Sweet Home

If you go and look around the area where you live, you will see plants and living creatures in many different places. Some plants grow in pavements; on walls and even occasionally in tarmac roads. The places where plants and animals live are called habitats, even a crack in the tarmac can be a habitat.

A truly wild habitat is one where there has been no interference from human beings. In the UK and North America there are very few truly wild habitats left. Peat bogs are a truly wild habitat. So too are tropical rainforests.

Over hundreds of years people have cut down trees, drained marshes, dug peat and planted fields. This has led to a lot of wild habitats being destroyed and new artificial ones being created.

## Hedgerows

If you look at a hedgerow carefully you will see that a lot of animals and plants live near or among it. Many of Britain's wild-flowers rely on hedgerows as home. In the last 50 years at least 160,000 km of hedgerows have been destroyed.

They have been removed mainly to make room for bigger fields to cope with modern farming methods which use large machines and fewer workers.

## Barn Owls

The barn owl, one of the most beautiful birds in Britain, often hunts by flying low over hedges, usually in the late evening or early morning. The owl is looking for voles that live in the long grass at the side of the hedge. The barn owl is now becoming quite rare, probably because of the lack of suitable habitats for voles.

*Above*: The barn owl is the farmer's friend but now it is a rare sight in the British countryside.

*Right*: Land being drained in Lancashire prior to commercial peat cutting. 2.5 million cubic metres of peat is used in Britain every year.

# Getting Out Of The Bog

What do you think of when you hear the word 'bog'? A wet, soggy and dangerous place where wandering strangers can get sucked into the mire? You would be quite wrong. Bogs are fascinating places which are home to some of the most beautiful and unusual plants and animals in the country.

## Getting Out The Bog

Bogs are made of layers and layers of moss, one layer growing on top of the other. The living surface holds rainwater. The water of the bog is very acidic (vinegar like) and pickles the moss after it has died. Pickled moss is called peat and it is widely used by gardeners.

## Nature Conservation

Here is a list of some of the plants and animals found in bogs:

*Insects* - include the white-faced dragonfly, giant raft spiders and even a beetle that, until recently, was only known to scientists from fossilised remains from the iron age!

*Birds* - include dunlin, plover, short-eared owl, hen-harriers and sparrow-hawks.

*Plants* - include the beautiful bog rosemary and sundews which are plants with sticky leaves that trap and devour insects.

## The Disappearing Bogs

Peat has been used by people for thousands of years. Today, however, peat is being used in huge quantities for gardening and horticulture. So much is being cut, using huge machines, that peat bogs are rapidly being destroyed.

Some of these bogs are nature reserves or places specially reserved for wildlife.

## Bog People

The water of bogs is so good at preserving things that several perfectly preserved human bodies have been found. In one or two cases the people who discovered them called the police but in fact the bodies are thousands of years old.

## What Can You Do?

Persuade people in your family to use an alternative to peat. Here are a few:

*Bark*
Stripped from felled trees and sold in bags.

*Leaf Mould*
The traditional ingredient in compost.

*Animal Manure*
Composted with straw.

*Sewage Sludge*
This makes an excellent, harmless and smell-free compost after it has been properly treated.

*Compost*
See the section on making your own compost heap.

*Above*: an expanse of devastated mossland.
*Left*: A dragonfly: just one of the rich variety of species found around bog land.

# BOTTLE GARDEN

Many house plants will grow happily in a transparent container placed on a light window sill.
All you need to make your garden in a bottle.
are —

MAKE YOUR OWN SELF-CONTAINED HABITAT FOR PLANTS.

Mosses grown in a small jar.

① A large transparent jar with a wide mouth.

A sweet jar is good,

a coffee jar

or a specially designed bottle garden jar.

② A lid

or cork

Which fits tightly.

③ Some fine stones or grit.

④ Some damp non-peat compost.

⑤ A spoon with a stick tied to the handle.

⑥ 2 or 3 kinds of slow growing house plants.

Tradescantia     Begonia     African violet

small ferns     Aluminium plant     Spider plant

**NOW —**

ⓐ Clean and dry the jar. Cover the bottom with a layer of grit.

for drainage

↑ 2½ cm. ↓ DEEP

ⓑ Use the extended spoon to put a layer of damp compost over the grit.

↑ 5 cm. ↓ DEEP

ⓒ Scoop out holes in the compost and spoon your plants into place.

firm the soil around their roots.

ⓓ Seal the container

and put in a position with plenty of light.

The jar should only need watering once a month

Steve Weatherill

# Going Wild

Have you ever seen a fox or even a badger in a street? We tend to think of towns and cities as being specially designed for people, not wildlife. However, many people find towns congested, polluted and noisy places while some wildlife seem to enjoy towns! Indeed, some animals such as house sparrows, rats and house mice use the human environment for their survival.

Pigeons, starlings, kestrels and foxes have all managed to find a home in the town. The wild ancestors of pigeons are the rock doves which nest on cliffs. For urban pigeons the tall buildings with their parapets make an ideal place for building their nests. Starlings find the extra heat of the cities keeps them warm during the winter time. Starlings roost in the cities at night and move into the country during the day to feed. Kestrels, like pigeons, find good nesting sites on the top of tall buildings where they can stay undisturbed. Foxes have become used to living close to people in towns and cities. They make their homes and rear their young in wooded, suburban gardens.

These are animals which make the most of the habitat provided by us. But there are better ways of making the urban environment attractive to wildlife - and attractive to us too.

In many places, people have gathered together to form urban wildlife groups which find urban wastelands and turn them into small wild environments in the middle of the city. Next to King's Cross Station in the heart of London is Camley Natural Park which was created from a derelict site. Here people can visit and experience at first hand wild birds, amphibians, and insects. Unfortunately, the park is threatened by redevelopment associated with the Channel Tunnel.

Some people from

Hans Reinhard / Tony Stone Worldwide

## Do Something!

● If you want to get involved write to the National Federation of City Farms or the Royal Society for Nature Conservation (see page 63) for details of your nearest city farm or urban wildlife scheme.

You could also get in touch with the British Trust for Conservation Volunteers - see the end of this book.

the inner cities have little contact with animals such as cows and sheep. So city farms have been set up to allow people to have the chance of direct contact with animals.

Those of us who live in the urban environment can help to improve it, both for ourselves and for wildlife. It only takes a little imagination, money and effort. The urban environment need not be the unpleasant place it may seem.

*Left*: A young fox. Foxes have become used to living close to people.

*Above*: Two sparrows find that an old gutter makes a sheltered habitat.

TRY AND SPOT THE TEN DIFFERENCES BETWEEN THESE PICTURES...

# Wildlife Garden
One way that you can really play an active part in protecting the environment is by starting your own wildlife garden. Wildlife gardens are good fun and you can learn a lot from watching them develop. If you don't have any garden yourself you could encourage your school to start one (away from areas where children play).

This picture is meant to give you some ideas as to how you could build a small wildlife garden, you don't need to use every idea; if you only use a few it will still encourage wildlife.

**Trees**. An Oak will feed more wildlife than any other tree but takes 30 years to grow. Mountain Ash and Alder grow far quicker and both produce a good crop of fruit for wildlife as well as being of a size that will fit into most people's gardens

Bird box

**Hedges**. A mixed hedge will encourage the most wildlife. Hawthorn makes a good, prickly, base; it has lots of berries on in the autumn. A Buddleia will encourage butterflies (pick a dwarf variety otherwise it could grow bigger than you expect).

**Wood and rubble piles**. A pile of twigs and small branches will encourage insects and beetles, and therefore insect-eating birds too. Rubble such as old bricks and stones can provide useful hiding places for insects; but also encourages lizards and slow-worm. Place these piles in shade — they can be hidden in an otherwise unused corner

Bird bath

**Plants**. If you have some bare ground with poor infertile soil, this is probably ideal for growing cornfield annuals such as Corn Marigold, Corn Cockle and Corn Flower. Wild flowers such as Cowslip, Campion or Oxeye will grow quite happily among grass (as long as you avoid putting fertilizer or chemicals down).

**For butterflies, moths and bees**. Nicotinia, Phlox and Wall flowers will all encourage pollinating insects. Honeysuckle encourages moths, and lavender is a plant that the bees just love

**Ponds**. These can be expensive and difficult to maintain as well as taking up quite a lot of space. They do, however, help encourage quite a lot of wildlife as well as being interesting. If you don't have much space an old stone sink makes quite a good pond. Most fish and water life prefers areas out of direct sunlight

# A Growing Concern!

Although you may not realise it, farming plays an important part in our daily lives. Not only does most of our food come from farms, but such things as leather for shoes, cotton and wool for clothes, and hessian for sacks come from farms either in Britain or abroad.

For the last 50 years farmers have produced more and more. They have been able to do this using artificial fertilizers to help their plants grow. They have also used pesticides to kill insect pests, and 'intensive' methods, such as factory farming, for keeping animals Although this has meant more food than ever before, many modern farming methods have harmed the environment.

Using pesticides, for example, not only causes pollution, but some of the chemicals end up in foodstuffs too. Many fertilizers have also caused damage. Nitrogen is one of the main foods that all plants need to grow. Nitrogen in most fertilizer is held in a form called nitrate. This nitrate is easily dissolved and often gets washed out of the soil into rivers and underground water where it can cause damage (nitrates can remain in underground water for many years).

Modern farming has damaged many wildlife habitats. Enough hedges have been removed in the last 50 years to go six times round the earth (at least 160,000 kilometres).

Many countries in Europe produce far more food than they need to feed their own people. Some countries have stored huge amounts of food in giant warehouses, or have sold it off cheaply to other countries. In Britain, farmers have been paid money to grow nothing on their land. This idea has been called "set aside", so one field can be left with nothing on it while the next is still farmed using chemicals. Farmers could also reduce their yields by using less nitrogen fertilizer.

Farms have become bigger since 1945 and many small farms have disappeared. Once, most farmers used to change the crops that they grew by rotation - using this method a different crop is grown in a field each year. This helps prevent diseases and helps the soil keep its 'goodness' or fertility. Today many farms grow only one crop, year after year. Doing this makes their crops even more likely to become diseased or get attacked by pests so farmers have often ended up using more and more chemicals.

It is possible to grow food by what is known as organic methods. Organic farmers do not use artificial chemicals or fertilizer, instead they use natural manures and rotations to help them grow their crops. This method of farming helps protect the environment because it is usually far less harmful to wildlife.

If we wish to preserve the countryside we need to develop ways of farming that fit in far more with nature. Farmers could use rotation more, and use less chemicals.

Some farmers look after the environment as well as growing crops, if more farmers were encouraged to follow their lead the countryside would be a safer place for wildlife and all of us would benefit.

*Below*: A helicopter sprays a field of crops with chemicals that can drift on to the surrounding countryside.

## Factory farming

Some animals are kept in very cramped conditions, so that they cannot move properly. Battery hens, for example, live in small cages. The lights are kept on for 23 hours a day so that the hens will lay more. Often huge numbers of animals are kept in enormous houses. This type of farming is called factory farming. Pigs for pork and bacon are also often kept in factory conditions. By contrast, free-range hens are allowed outside to peck and feed. Free-range hens produce more eggs in the summer, when the days are longer, than they do in the winter.

*Above*: compare these free-range chickens to the battery hens (*inset*). There's little doubt which *they* prefer.
*Right*: factory farmed pigs.

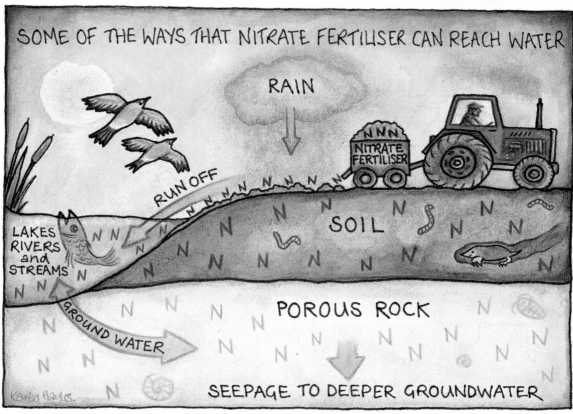

SOME OF THE WAYS THAT NITRATE FERTILISER CAN REACH WATER

RAIN

NITRATE FERTILISER

RUN OFF

SOIL

LAKES RIVERS and STREAMS

GROUND WATER

POROUS ROCK

SEEPAGE TO DEEPER GROUNDWATER

## Biological control

Some types of insect pest are not killed by the poisons sprayed on foods any more. They have become resistant to the chemicals. A little pest called whitefly that attacks greenhouse plants such as tomatoes, has become resistant to so many chemicals that very few poisons kill it any more. For this reason, growers have started using another insect - a tiny wasp that you can hardly see, called Encarsia Formosa. The lava (or grub) of this insect eats the whitefly before it fully develops. By releasing these little flying insects it is possible to get rid of whitefly in a natural way without chemicals. Many growers now use this method to control whitefly. This method is called 'biological control'.

Left: Michael Kornafel / Tony Stone Worldwide
Inset and below left: Animal Aid

Illustration below: John Davey

### Do something!

● Ask people in your family to consider buying organic food and free-range eggs.

● If you live in the countryside on a farm, you could consider fitting an owl box on a local barn.

## The Friendly Worm

Earthworms are very important in the garden. They help break down and mix dead and rotting bits of leaves and plant material with the soil.

By making a wormery you will be able to see for yourself the way a worm mixes the soil. As well as helping the gardener, worms are a useful source of food for wildlife such as birds, badgers and hedgehogs. After you have finished with your wormery release the worms back into the garden so that they can keep on doing good.

**Note** — Even though earthworms are tickly in your hand, they are absolutely harmless. They carry no disease and cannot in any way hurt you. So, friendly really is the right word for the worm.

1. Take a large jam jar with a lid. Put some pebbles at the bottom for drainage then half fill the jar with loose soil

Soil
Stones

2. Gently put two earth-worms in the jar

Leaves and bark

3. Put some leaves and bits of bark on top of the soil.

4. Wrap a piece of black paper around the jar. This keeps it dark and the worms will then build their tunnels against the glass. Worms avoid light because it can harm them.

Air holes

5. Put a lid on the jar but first make some air holes in it. Also, spray the leaves and soil with water every now and then then. Keep the jar in a cool place.

6. Observe what happens. You'll see the bark and leaves dis-appear as the worms break them down. You'll also see the worms tunnel against the glass.

WORM RECORD SHEET

# A Load Of Rubbish

Have you ever thought about all the stuff that is thrown away in your home? You may think that it's all a load of rubbish but the chances are that you are getting rid of a lot of valuable material.

In Britain, we throw away 26 million tonnes of household waste each year and 23 and a half million tonnes of this ends up in holes in the ground called landfill sites. Burying waste in the ground doesn't help the environment. The decaying waste produces gases such as methane which escape into the atmosphere and contribute to global warming. The waste can also pollute the water in the ground which runs into streams and rivers and eventually becomes our drinking water. Also, we're running out of suitable landfill sites.

Some waste is burnt in special containers called incinerators. This method of waste disposal solves the landfill site problem but it gives off gases that can cause air pollution if they are not 'cleaned'. In Denmark, 75 per cent of waste is burnt and the heat given off is used as energy for heating homes and factories.

## Valuable Resources

Metal, glass, paper, plastic, food all of these waste items are resources. Rather than throwing them all out we can re-use or recycle them. For example, vegetable waste can be put on a compost heap; (see: 'How to make a compost heap' P.30).

Waste is expensive - it costs time, energy and money to dispose of it. But we still create an awful lot! Each year, every person in Britain throws away, on average:

* 90 drink cans

* 107 bottles and jars

* 45 kg of plastics

* 70 food cans

* 2 trees worth of paper

* 140 kg of food waste

Aluminium, steel and glass can be taken to can and bottle banks and paper to waste paper collections. At the moment, there are few schemes to collect plastic for recycling but you can help the environment by buying glass bottles rather than plastic whenever you can.

## Cardiff - Recycling City

Cardiff is set to be the first UK city to recycle over half of its rubbish.

As part of Friends of the Earth's Recycling City project, Cardiff will have door-to-door collections of glass, paper, cans, glass and plastic, which will all be recycled.

The rubbish left over will be 'anaerobically digested' - rotted down to give methane gas for fuel, and compost for gardens.

There will also be mini-recycling centres all around the city, so that visitors to Cardiff can join in too.

### Chop Chop

In Japan, environmentalists held a National Chopsticks Day to protest against the 20 billion pairs of disposable wooden chopsticks that are used and thrown away each year, and encourage their re-use.

WASTE WORDSQUARE

THESE WORDS ARE HIDDEN IN THE WORDSQUARE CAN YOU FIND THEM?

BOTTLEBANK — TIN
LITTER — DUSTBIN
RECYCLING — WASTE
PAPER — DECOMPOSE
RUBBISH — GLASS
POLLUTION — ROT

## Do Something!

● Watch your waste! Put everything you throw away (apart from food waste) over a day, or maybe 2 or 3 days into a large cardboard box or your recycling robot. How much is metal, paper, card or plastic? How much could be recycled or re-used for something? Now try the same experiment but really try to cut down on buying unnecessary packaging. How much lands up in your box now?

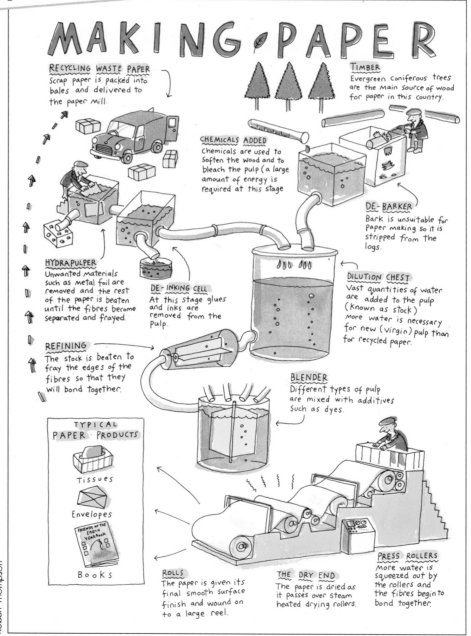

# MAKING PAPER

**RECYCLING WASTE PAPER**
Scrap paper is packed into bales and delivered to the paper mill.

**TIMBER**
Evergreen coniferous trees are the main source of wood for paper in this country.

**CHEMICALS ADDED**
Chemicals are used to soften the wood and to bleach the pulp (a large amount of energy is required at this stage)

**DE-BARKER**
Bark is unsuitable for paper making so it is stripped from the logs.

**HYDRAPULPER**
Unwanted materials such as metal foil are removed and the rest of the paper is beaten until the fibres become separated and frayed.

**DE-INKING CELL**
At this stage glues and inks are removed from the pulp.

**DILUTION CHEST**
Vast quantities of water are added to the pulp (known as stock) More water is necessary for new (virgin) pulp than for recycled paper.

**REFINING**
The stock is beaten to fray the edges of the fibres so that they will bond together.

**BLENDER**
Different types of pulp are mixed with additives such as dyes.

**TYPICAL PAPER·PRODUCTS**
Tissues
Envelopes
FRIENDS OF THE EARTH YEARBOOK
Books

**ROLLS**
The paper is given its final smooth surface finish and wound on to a large reel.

**THE DRY END**
The paper is dried as it passes over steam heated drying rollers.

**PRESS ROLLERS**
More water is squeezed out by the rollers and the fibres begin to bond together.

Robert Thompson

28

# The Short Life of a Plastic Bottle

The bottle leaves the factory

↓

It is filled with a drink

↓

It is bought and the contents drunk

↓

The empty bottle is put in the waste bin

↓

**It is dumped in a landfill site and
buried, where it lasts and lasts**

Roger Hiorns

## The Life of a Milk Bottle

The bottle leaves the glass factory
and goes to the dairy...

The milkman
takes it back
to the dairy
where it is
washed

The bottle is
filled / refilled
with milk

The empty
bottle is
left on the
doorstep

Delivered
by the
milkman

Mmmm - cornflakes
and milk'

The five R's of waste

-EFUSE to be given unnecessary packaging.

-ETURN bottles whenever you can; buy
returnable bottles if possible.

-EUSE as many envelopes and plastic bags as
you can. Take unwanted clothes to charity shops.

-EPAIR rather than throw away.

-ECYCLE paper, cans and bottles by taking
them to your local recycling centre. Ask
your local council where it is.

RECYCLING CENTRE

Lesley McGibbon

# RECYCLE YOUR WASTE-MAKE A COMPOST HEAP

One third of the average dustbin is kitchen and garden waste.

Most of this could be turned back into soil by making a compost heap.

**1** Find a sunny place at the bottom of the garden, sheltered from the wind.

Sorry dad, but we need this spot for the compost heap.

**2** You will need 4 stakes
A length of wire netting
1½m — 6 metres — 2 metres
Some nails and staples

**3** Knock the stakes into the ground and surround with wire netting.

**4** Line with old carpet or cardboard to keep the heap warm.

**5** Start with a layer of prunings and stalks. They help to supply air to the bottom of the heap.

**6** Next put on a layer of grass cuttings and leaves. Build up a layer at a time. Tread down well.

SOIL

tea leaves
potato peelings
egg shells
leaves
grass cuttings
twigs prunings

MINIMUM SIZE 1½ METRES SQUARE

END OF WIRE NETTING IS HOOKED OVER BENT NAILS FOR EASY ACCESS.

**7** The middle of the heap will start to heat up as bacteria and micro-organisms rot it down.

**8** Cover the top with a layer of soil. Water every 2 weeks if dry.

**10** In about 3 months you should have a rich manure ready to add to and improve your garden soil.

**9** Turn the heap over with a fork after about 6 weeks. This will speed up the composting.

Steve Weatherill

# ROBOT RECYCLER

You can make your own recycling monster. Use him to store paper and other material, but not glass, for recycling.

YOU'LL NEED_

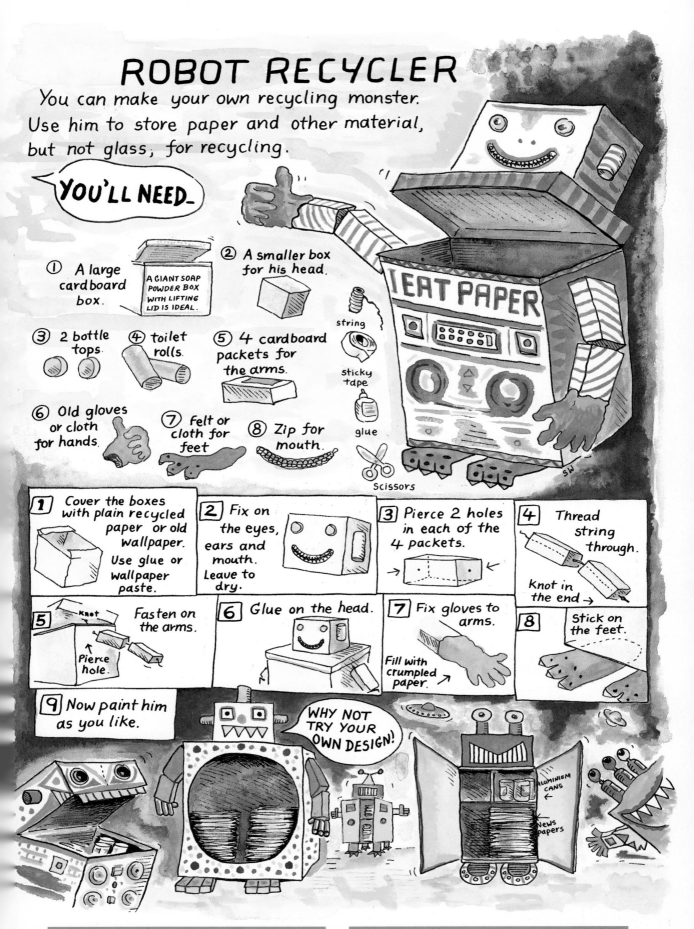

① A large cardboard box.

A GIANT SOAP POWDER BOX WITH LIFTING LID IS IDEAL.

② A smaller box for his head.

③ 2 bottle tops.

④ toilet rolls.

⑤ 4 cardboard packets for the arms.

string

sticky tape

glue

⑥ Old gloves or cloth for hands.

⑦ Felt or cloth for feet

⑧ Zip for mouth.

Scissors

**1** Cover the boxes with plain recycled paper or old wallpaper. Use glue or wallpaper paste.

**2** Fix on the eyes, ears and mouth. Leave to dry.

**3** Pierce 2 holes in each of the 4 packets.

**4** Thread string through. Knot in the end →

**5** Fasten on the arms. Knot. Pierce hole.

**6** Glue on the head.

**7** Fix gloves to arms. Fill with crumpled paper →

**8** Stick on the feet.

**9** Now paint him as you like.

WHY NOT TRY YOUR OWN DESIGN!

ALUMINIUM CANS

News papers

# Going Places

You may have seen the car sticker with the smiling child and the proud motto: "Go Green - Use Lead Free". As lead harms the development of children's brains, it is good news that its use in petrol is declining. But does anyone really have any reason to smile?

Lead is only one of the poisonous ingredients in petrol. Cars also put into the air:

* Carbon monoxide, which, like lead, can damage the brains of unborn children.

* Benzines, which can cause cancer. More benzine is produced by super-unleaded, the so called green petrol!

* Carbon dioxide, which is the main cause of the greenhouse effect. On average, a car produces four times its own weight in carbon dioxide each year.

* Nitrogen oxides which cause acid rain; killing forests and lakes.

Even without lead, car and lorry fumes will continue to damage our health and the environment. It has been estimated that fumes from motor vehicles lead to the deaths of 30,000 people in the United States each year.

Cars do not only pollute the air; in Britain 5,000 people are killed every year in road accidents. Cars also make cycling and walking difficult. Many people become afraid of roads.

*Left*: Motorway madness. Many car journeys can be avoided and goods can be transported by train.

*Above*: Commuters walk to work over **London Bridge**.

## Bike It - why cycles are good

*Cycling is a great, healthy, fun and cheap form of exercise and it's good for the environment, but roads can be very dangerous. You can help yourself to stay safe by following these useful tips:*

★ Check your bike regularly, especially the wheels, brakes and lights.

★ Wear something fluorescent during the day and something reflective at night. Always use your lights at night.

★ Try to avoid busy roads and junctions. Watch out for other road users, they may do something unexpected.

★ Contact the road safety department of your local council for details of training courses in your area.

With more and more cars on the road, life for people without a motor vehicle often becomes difficult. Getting about by such things as buses and trains (public transport) gets worse. Shops and schools are built further and further away from people's homes.

## The Solutions

Protecting the environment means making careful choices. Here are some ideas.

* Don't build roads: Although we spend billions of pounds on road-building, knocking down thousands of homes and tarmacing green spaces, traffic jams become more and more

common. This is because new roads create new traffic, by tempting people to switch from public transport to their cars.

* Improve public transport. Travelling by buses and trains uses far less energy per person, and also produces far less pollution. The more people use public transport, the less roads will be blocked up with cars.

* The government needs to improve public transport so that it is more comfortable and services are regular. This would encourage people to use it.

* Many cities in Europe have decided that it is very damaging to allow cars freely on the road that they have stopped people using cars in certain places and at certain times - this is called traffic restraint. In some cities, they have put special electronic gadgets in cars and at the roadside and the driver has to pay something for every mile she or he travels. This helps prevent blocked up roads and allows extra space for people on foot and

cyclists as well as freeing bus and bike lanes.

## Road Facts

When public transport was greatly improved in London in 1983 and 1984, the number of people travelling to work by car decreased by 21% and the number of people using the tube increased by 44%. It was estimated that the reduction in car traffic meant 3,500 fewer road casualties in 1983 alone.

### Do something!
* Encourage people at home to use public transport, and walk when there is only a short distance to travel.
* If you know of a dangerous road write a letter to your local council asking them to do something about it.

# What's Green and Powerful?

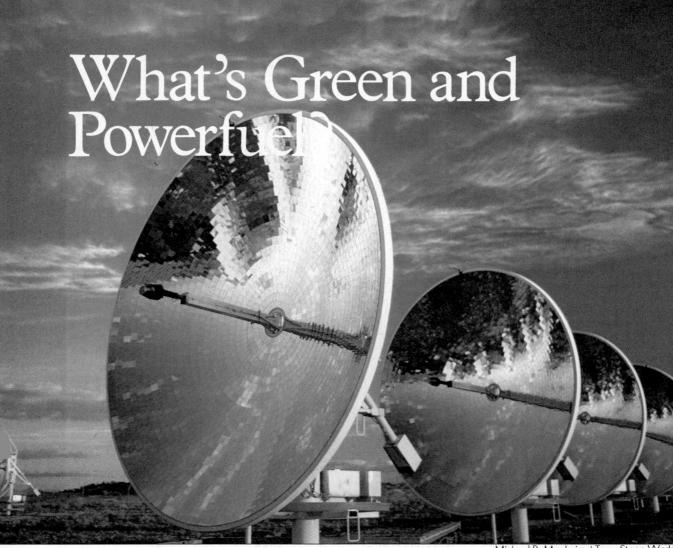

Michael P. Manheim / Tony Stone World

If you boiled water in a kettle this morning, had a cooked breakfast, used warm water, put on a light, a heater or a radio, or used transport, you used energy. We cannot do without it - but we *can* use it more carefully.

Alex Olah / Environmental Picture library

**An oil rig extracts oil from the North Sea bed. Where will our energy come from when fossil fuel runs out?**

The wealthier, developed countries such as Britain and the United States use a lot of energy, much more than the less developed parts of the world. An average family in the UK uses 80 times more energy than an average family in Africa.

The huge amounts of energy we use are causing major problems for the environment. In general, the more energy we use the more pollution we create. Most of our energy is produced by burning fossil fuels such as coal, oil and gas, often to make electricity. Burning these fuels pollutes the atmosphere, causes problems such as acid rain and contributes to global warming (see P.42). Once fossil fuels have been used up that's it! It takes millions of years for new ones to form.

Nuclear power is also used as a source of electrical energy. Many people think that it is unsafe and costs too much money. In 1986 an explosion at Chernobyl nuclear power plant in the Soviet Union resulted in a cloud of radioactive dust spreading over most of western Europe. 135,000 people had to be evacuated from their homes

Tony Stone Worldwide

**Wind farms can be beautiful as well as green.**

### SAVE YOUR ENERGY!

A lot of energy is wasted. Most light bulbs, for instance, get very hot because they are using energy to make heat as well as light; but we only want the light - the heat is useless. There are light bulbs that stay far cooler but still produce the same amount of light, these use less electricity and are called energy efficient bulbs.

We also need to use less energy through energy conservation. Many homes lose energy through not insulating buildings properly. This can be done by putting a layer of material (fibre glass and rock wool are often used) in lofts and in the gap or cavity in walls. Energy can also be saved by stopping draughts that come through badly fitting doors and windows.

A lot of heat is lost in factories and industry - it simply goes out of the chimney. In coal burning power stations, less than 40 per cent of the energy released from the coal is made into electricity - most of the rest is lost as heat from the cooling towers.

Recycling waste also helps save energy. The energy required to produce recycled paper is half the amount needed to produce newpaper.

immediately and an area of 2800 square metres is now unfit for people to live in for many years to come. This is larger than many English counties.

Nuclear power stations constantly produce a large amount of waste which is very difficult to get rid of because it remains radioactive, and therefore potentially dangerous, for thousands of years.

There are forms

# HOW TO MAKE A WINDMILL

You can capture the wind's energy for yourself with this simple model of a wind generator.

**① You will need —**
a cork bung (used for winemaking)
hole
a 2½" nail
4 pins
a stick (50 cm long)
a sheet of thin card

**② Cut out a cardboard washer.**
Put nail through the hole in the cork.

**③ Knock into the top of the stick.**
Make sure it spins ᵗˡˡ( freely )〉〉〉〉

**④ Push pins into the sides of the cork—**
—Opposite each other and set at an angle.

**⑤ Now cut out two fins from the card.**
10–15 cm
fin

**⑥ Tape them to the pins and try it out.**
You will find that the angle of the fins makes a difference to the speed and direction of spin.
Try different shapes and positions for the fins.
You will probably have to spend some time adjusting the fins to get the windmill working at its best.

Steve Weatherill

of energy which will not run out and are safer and cleaner. These are called renewable sources of energy and they use the power of the wind, waves, tides and sun, or the heat deep within the Earth's crust. Renewable energy is being used all around the world in windmills, solar panels and hydroelectric dams. However, these sources still supply only a small part of all the energy we use.

It is important that we do not waste the energy we produce. If we want to protect the environment we will need to develop ways of using energy effectively as well as producing it cleanly.

Mike Abrahams / Tony Stone Worldwide

*Above*: A miner digs coal from a narrow shaft.

## Do something!

● **Save energy when you can - switch off heaters, lights or any other electrical appliances if you're not using them.**

● **Put on an extra sweater rather than turning on a heater.**

● **Carry out the home energy survey and tell the people you live with what they could be doing to save energy - and money on the bills!**

● **Walk, cycle or use public transport when you can and if it's safe to do so.**

# Home Energy Survey

Conduct this survey in your home - you can answer some of the questions by yourself but you could also interview the people at home.

*1. Are there any draughts coming through*

a) the outside doors?
b) outside windows?
c) letterbox?

**Scores**:
1 a) b) & c) Score 5 for each NO

*2. Is there any insulation*

a) in the loft?
b) in the walls?

**Scores**:
2 a) Score 10 for YES
b) Score 5 for YES

*3. Are there any*

a) lights
b) heaters

*switched on in rooms that are not being used?*

**Scores**:
3. a) Score 5 for NO
b) Score 10 for NO

*4. Are the windows double glazed?*

**Scores**:
4. Score 10 for YES

*5. Do you shower more than you bath?*

**Scores**:
5. Score 10 for YES

*6. Would you put on an extra sweater rather than turn up the heating?*

**Scores**:
6. Score 20 for YES

**TOTAL SCORE:**

YOUR SCORE:
*Score 50-75*  You really know how to save energy and money on fuel bills.

*Score 25-50*  You are saving some energy but look around and see what else you can do.

*Score under 25*  There's a lot more that can be done. Ask for advice from the Energy Efficiency Office (address at the end of the book)

---

## DOES INSULATION WORK?

Take two jam jars.

1. Place one in a small box surrounded by some insulating material such as cotton wool, clothing, rags, or newspaper. Make sure it is packed tight in the box.

2. Leave the second jam jar unwrapped.

3. Fill both jars with the same amount of hot water.

4. After half an hour compare the temperature of the two jars. Can you explain the difference?

# Shopping for a Greener World

Everyone can help make the world a better place by being careful about what they buy.

Look on the shelves of your local supermarket: the number of products claiming to be better for the environment is enormous. Ozone-friendly aerosols, phosphate-free washing powders, organic vegetables... the list is endless.

Some manufacturers claim that their products are good for the environment just to try to sell them. Others have made a real attempt to change. So how can you tell which is which?

The other sections of this book should give you some clues. See for example the Five R's Of Waste on page 29. Here are just a few useful tips.

* Avoid buying wood from tropical rainforests.

* Use recycled paper.

* Avoid over-wrapped goods.

* Buy milk in returnable bottles.

* Encourage people at home to buy energy efficient electrical goods.

* Avoid using aerosols if possible. All aerosols are wasteful of resources even though most don't now contain CFC's. If possible buy pump action refillable sprays.

* Ask people at home to avoid purchasing artificial garden chemicals.

* Encourage people at home to buy organically grown food where it is available.

* Don't believe all the claims that manufacturers make. Work out if they are true for yourself.

For more detailed information, Friends of the Earth have produced a leaflet on Green Consumerism.

## The Green Con Award

Friends of the Earth have set up an award for manufacturers who try to claim the public with their advertising. In 1989 British Nuclear Fuels won it with their advert which claimed that nuclear power was 'green'. If you have some nominations for the green con award why don't you let us have them. By showing that manufacturers are not being honest in their claims, we hope that it is possible to put others off making them in the future.

*Above right*: Washing up - no-one's favourite job but stop and ask whether all washing up liquids are as green as they claim. *Above centre*: The soil association symbol guarantees that this product is organically grown.

We're Getting Warmer

Our biggest environmental threat is *global warming*, caused by the greenhouse effect. Have you ever been in a garden greenhouse? It's warmer inside than out because the glass stops a lot of the warmth from the sun from escaping. The atmosphere surrounding the Earth works in a similar way by trapping some of the Sun's energy. This keeps the Earth warm enough for plants and animals to live, but now too much warmth is being trapped because of pollution.

cooler and too cold for life. But now, we are upsetting the balance.

Over the past 100 years, people have been using more and more energy as many countries have increased their industry. Most of the energy comes from fossil fuels such as coal, oil and gas.

## Greenhouse Gases

The atmosphere is mainly made of nitrogen and oxygen gases but also tiny amounts of other gases such as carbon dioxide ($CO_2$), methane, ozone and CFCs (see page 56). About 30 of these other gases are called the 'greenhouse gases' because they act rather like glass in a greenhouse, trapping in heat. The greenhouse gases are important in balancing the Earth's temperature. They allow heat energy (short-wave *radiation*) from the Sun to reach and warm the planet surface but stop some of the heat energy (long-wave radiation) that is reflected back from Earth from escaping out to space. This trapped radiation warms the planet. Without it the Earth would be over 30° C

Vanessa Miles / Environmental Picture library

When fossil fuels are burnt - for example in cars, factories and to make electricity, they give off carbon dioxide ($CO_2$), one of the greenhouse gases. This is the key cause of global warming but other human activities also increase the greenhouse gases in the atmosphere - the burning of huge areas of tropical forests adds to $CO_2$ levels and increasing amounts of methane gas are being produced. Methane is given off by animals such as cattle (or humans!) and also by vegetation rotting in swamps and rice paddy fields. It is hard to believe that cattle, rice fields and forests can make a difference but there are millions of cattle, millions of hectares of rice paddies, and millions of hectares of forests being cut down. Planting more trees and halting the destruction of the rainforests would help to reduce the amount of carbon dioxide in the atmosphere.

## Warming

The increase in greenhouse gases means that less heat energy goes out into space and the world becomes warmer. This is called *global warming*

Martin Bond / Environmental Picture library

and it is estimated that the Earth's temperature could rise by between 1.5° C and 4.5° C within 50 years. This may not seem a large temperature rise but scientists predict that global warming could cause big changes in the world's weather patterns. They also say the oceans will expand, raising sea levels and flooding many low-lying areas.

There is still uncertainty about the amount of global warming there will be, and what effects it will have, but most scientists agree that we urgently need to reduce the amount of pollution - particularly carbon dioxide - we are putting into the atmosphere.

## Global Releaf

Global Releaf is the name of a campaign launched by the American Forestry Association. They aim to encourage Americans to plant 100 million new trees within 4 years.

*Previous page left*: The sun isn't getting hotter but greenhouse gases released into the atmosphere probably mean that the Earth is.

*Left*: Scientists predict that flooding could become more widespread as oceans expand.

## Do something!

● Get involved in tree planting. You could even start your own wildlife garden at home or school (see page 18). The Woodland Trust or the British Trust for Conservation Volunteers can help you. (See addresses at the end of the book.)

● Save and recycle paper - because paper is made from wood this will save the forests. Also, saving waste reduces rubbish going to landfill sites which can leak methane.

● Use your bike or public transport when you can. This helps cut carbon dioxide pollution.

Vanessa Miles / Environmental Picture Library

CARBON DIOXIDE, NITROGEN OXIDE, METHANE AND CFC GAS COLLECTS HIGH ABOVE THE EARTH'S SURFACE. IT ACTS LIKE A GREENHOUSE BY TRAPPING THE SUN'S HEAT REFLECTED BACK FROM THE EARTH AND MAKING THE ATMOSPHERE WARMER.

MOST ELECTRICITY IS PRODUCED BY BURNING FOSSIL FUELS, (COAL, OIL, GAS) WHICH GIVES OFF HUGE AMOUNTS OF **CARBON DIOXIDE**

MILLIONS OF CAR EXHAUSTS GIVING OUT **CARBON DIOXIDE** AND **NITRONS OXIDE.**

AS RUBBISH ROTS IT GIVES OFF **METHANE GAS.**

POWER STATIONS

RUBBISH DUMPS

CARS

Steve Weatherill

**46**

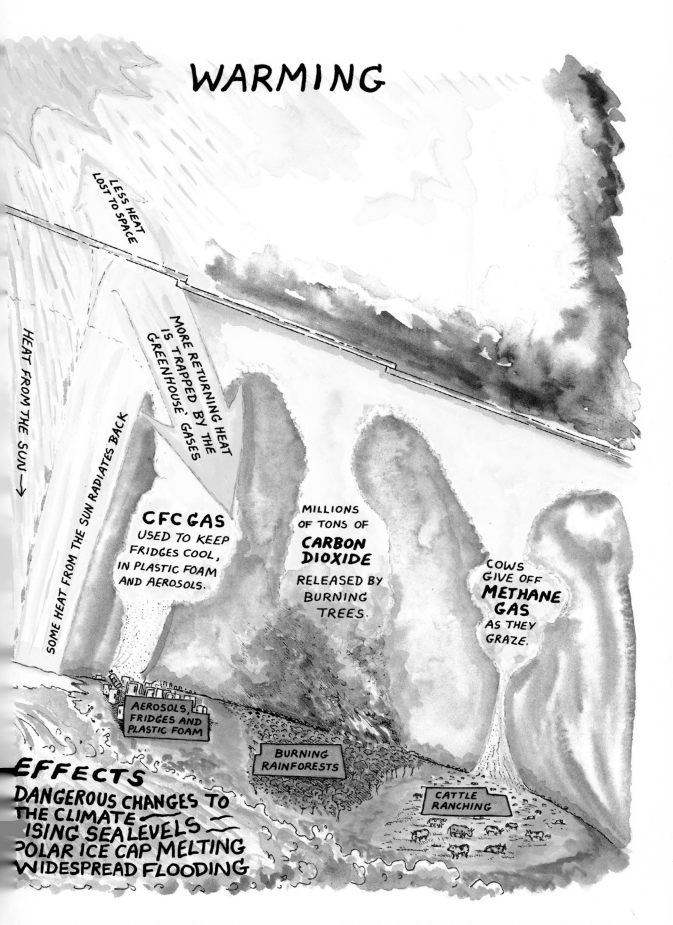

# You Must Be Choking!

If you watch smoke from a chimney, you will see how, on a still day, it rises high into the air and how, on a windy day, gets quickly mixed up and blown around. The smoke shows you how the air is moving. Although you can see smoke, many air pollutants are invisible and we can breathe them in without knowing. Air pollution can be carried for hundreds of kilometres by air currents.

As the number of people on the planet has grown and as factories and industrial sites have been developed, more and more pollutants have been put into the air causing air pollution. But it isn't just factories and power stations that are to blame; domestic fires, cigarettes and car exhausts also cause air pollution.

Acid rain is caused by air pollution, mainly from burning fossil fuels (coal, oil, natural gas) to make electricity. When fossil fuels are burnt the fumes contain a gas called sulphur dioxide ($SO_2$) and nitrogen oxides ($NO_x$). $SO_2$ and $NO_x$ enter the atmosphere and are carried by the wind. Some particles of the chemicals fall directly on to trees, lakes and soil but others mix with water vapour in the air to make a weak acid. This then falls to the ground as acid rain,

## AIR FACTS

☆ The air consists of 78per cent nitrogen, 21per cent oxygen, 1per cent other gases such as carbon dioxide, neon, argon.

☆ There are 550 million vehicles in the world today. Parked bumper-to-bumper, they would make a traffic queue that would go round the world 40 times.

☆ North America discharges 24 million tonnes of sulphur dioxide ($SO_2$) and 22 million tonnes of nitrogen oxides ($NO_x$) into the air each year. Europe discharges 44 million tonnes of $SO_2$ and 15 million of $NO_x$.

snow or mist. Some rain has been recorded that is as acidic as lemon juice.

Acid rain is damaging lakes, rivers, trees and buildings especially in Europe and North America where there has been industrial activity for over 100 years. Scandinavia is one of the worst affected areas in Europe. Air pollution is blown there from the industrial areas of Britain, West Germany and Eastern Europe. Many lakes are so acid that fish and insects cannot live in them and trees are weakened so that they cannot survive disease or high winds. The Swedish government has had to take drastic action, mixing tonnes of lime with the lake water to make it less acidic.

## Do something!

● Encourage people at home to use public transport more. Don't always ask to be driven in the car especially if it is a short, safe journey. Walk or cycle more. Fewer cars on the road means less nitrogen oxides and other pollutants in the atmosphere.

● Cut down on the amount of electricity you use by switching off lights and heaters when they're not being used. Saving energy reduces the amount of $SO_2$ and $NO_x$ sent into the air by power stations.

● Encourage adults to fit catalytic convertors to their cars, or buy cars with a catalytic convertor.

## Be a Pollution Detective!

How much pollution is there in your local area? This experiment will show the amount of visible pollutants in the air.

1. Glue or pin strips of sticky tape (sticky side out) onto several pieces of card or you can cover the pieces of card with a clear grease such as 'Vaseline'.

2. Put the pieces of card outside in the garden, or anywhere you wish to measure the air pollution. Pin them to a post or shed, but make sure they are in a place where they will not be disturbed and, if possible, are protected from the rain.

3. Keep one piece of card and put it in a place indoors where it will not be disturbed.

4. After one or two weeks, look at what has stuck to all the cards. Use a magnifying glass if you have one. Note the differences - which areas have most pollution, which direction does the wind usually blow. Can you identify the sources of any pollution.

*Previous page*: **The black smoke from this plant is very visible (*main pic.*) but other air pollutants are not so obvious (*inset*).**

*Left*: **Vast areas of forest land are under attack from acid rain.**

*Below*: **Coal fired power stations are a major source of sulphur dioxide: the main cause of acid rain.**

# Water Slaughter

<u>You use water every day: in drinks, for washing, perhaps for rinsing and cleaning. It's important stuff!</u>

If you stopped drinking water, you would die within three or four days. But the water we drink must be clean; it must be free of poisonous substances and germs that can harm us. Unclean drinking water can cause outbreaks of deadly diseases such as cholera.

Most of the water we drink comes from streams, rivers, lakes or from under the ground. Before we drink it, the water companies treat water to make sure it is safe and clean. Sometimes this is because they use similar chemicals to kill the germs that would make us ill. However, if our rivers and streams were cleaner, less treatment would be needed to be carried out by the water companies.

The main causes of water becoming polluted are sewage from towns and cities, chemicals used by farmers, waste from farm animals, and chemical wastes from industry. The animals and plants that live near or in the rivers and lakes also need clean water. But some of Britain's rivers are so polluted that little can live in them. Today, the National Rivers Authority is responsible for keeping our rivers clean. However, the record for prosecution is not good. Only 2% of water pollution incidents resulted in prosecution in 1988.

Tony Stone Worldwide

***Above and below***: **Clean river water contrasted against the polluted Humberside coastline.**

Alan Grieg / Environmental Picture Library

## FACTS - WATER

- 126 out of 600 bathing beaches in England and Wales are too dirty to use according to EEC guidelines.
- Millions of people in Britain are supplied with tap water which does not meet European Community standards.
- A gallon of oil spilt on water can cover an area twice the size of a football pitch.

Water isn't just for washing hands - every plant and animal on Earth needs water to live.

## The 'Thames Bubbler'

Thirty or forty years ago the tidal stretches of the River Thames were more or less dead - there were no fish and little water life. A massive clean-up operation took place over many years and today there are over 100 types of fish.

However, pollution still kills fish in the Thames. The main problem is sewage discharge. As pollutants break down they use up the oxygen in the water and the river suffers from 'oxygen sags' or areas where there is not enough oxygen for the animals and plants. To combat this, Thames Water have launched the Thames Bubbler, a ship which patrols the river pumping oxygen back into the river where it is needed - this helps the life support system for the river.

## Polluting the seas

The world's seas and oceans are also polluted. They are used as a 'dustbin' for millions of tons of waste chemicals and sewage. Also, oil leaks into the sea when ships, especially tankers, sink or crash. Friends of the Earth campaigns to clean-up the seas.

*Above*: A clean up campaign in south Devon after an oil spill from an offshore tanker, (May 1990). *Below*: Glacier water is polluted by domestic, industrial and farmyard waste as it travels to the sea.

### Do something!

● Don't use more water than you need. This saves water, causes less sewage and means fewer new reservoirs for holding water need to be built.

● Ask people in your family to recycle old car oil. This can be done through a garage that accepts oil for recycling.

● Contact WATCH (see address page) for details on testing streams for water pollution.

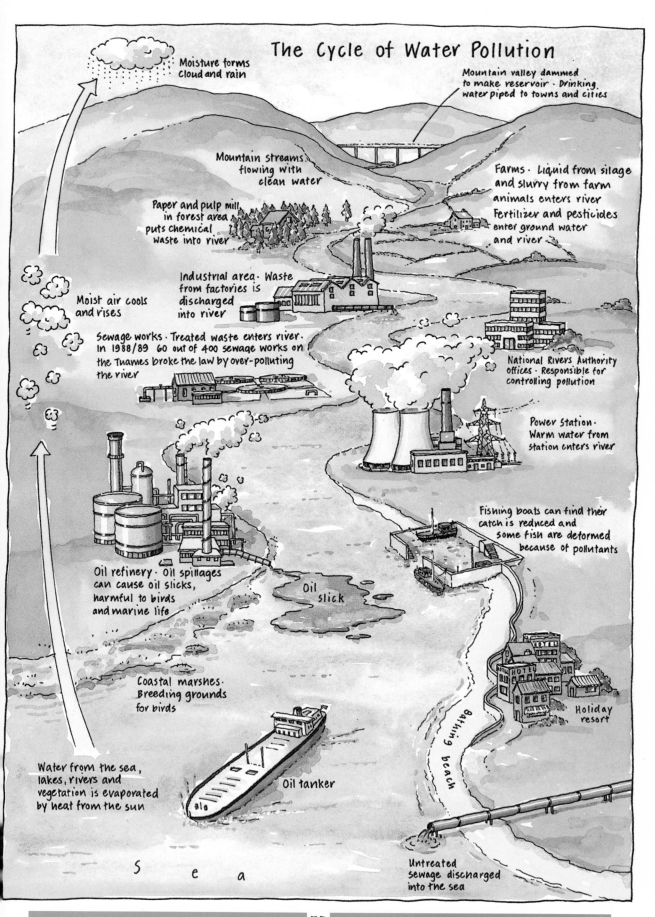

The Cycle of Water Pollution

Moisture forms cloud and rain

Mountain valley dammed to make reservoir. Drinking water piped to towns and cities

Mountain streams flowing with clean water

Farms. Liquid from silage and slurry from farm animals enters river. Fertilizer and pesticides enter ground water and river.

Paper and pulp mill in forest area puts chemical waste into river

Industrial area. Waste from factories is discharged into river

Moist air cools and rises

National Rivers Authority offices. Responsible for controlling pollution

Sewage works. Treated waste enters river. In 1988/89 60 out of 400 sewage works on the Thames broke the law by over-polluting the river

Power Station. Warm water from station enters river

Fishing boats can find their catch is reduced and some fish are deformed because of pollutants

Oil refinery. Oil spillages can cause oil slicks, harmful to birds and marine life

Oil slick

Coastal marshes. Breeding grounds for birds

Holiday resort

Water from the sea, lakes, rivers and vegetation is evaporated by heat from the sun

Oil tanker

Bathing beach

Sea

Untreated sewage discharged into the sea

# Blowing our Cover

We all like the Sun but not too much of it!

In 1985, scientists working in Antarctica discovered a 'hole' in the ozone layer. The hole was as big as the United States and it appeared every spring. Now there are signs that there will be a hole over the Arctic.

Ozone is found in a layer right around the Earth between 10 and 50 kilometres above sea level. The ozone layer is important because it absorbs 99 per cent of the damaging ultra-violet (UV) part of the Sun's light energy and prevents it reaching the Earth.

UV radiation can harm the growth of plants on land or in the sea which, in turn, affects the animals that feed on the plants as there is less to eat. This UV radiation can also cause eye diseases and skin cancer in humans if they are exposed to a lot of sunlight.

The ozone hole is caused by chemicals released into the atmosphere by humans. One of the worst group of these chemicals are called CFCs (chlorofluorocarbons). CFCs also contribute to the greenhouse effect (see page 42).

About thirty per cent of the world production of CFCs are used in fridges, freezers and air conditioners, while aerosols account for another 25 per cent. CFCs are also used to make some packaging (blown foam

cartons), foam insulation and fluids for cleaning computer parts.

The hole in the ozone layer and the possibility of an increase in UV radiation reaching the Earth is a global problem which needs international action. There have been some developments. In 1987 the Montreal Protocol was signed - it was the first ever truly global agreement on the environment but it only called for a 50 per cent cut in CFC consumption by the year 1999.

## Going ozone friendly

As the threat to the ozone layer has become known, there have been measures to reduce the amount of CFCs released into the air. Most manufacturers have stopped using CFCs to propel the contents in aerosols and have used alternative propellant gases. Better still, some have started producing pump-action sprays which need no propellant gas to make them work. The changes were largely due to the work carried out by Friends of the Earth in letting people know about the problems of CFCs.

Fridges and freezers are being developed that use less CFCs or different gases for their cooling and insulation systems. The city of Portsmouth has set up a CFC Gas Reclamation Service to collect and recycle CFCs from disused fridges and freezers.

Philip Carr / Environmental Picture Library

## FACTS - OZONE

* A one per cent decrease in total ozone can lead to a increase in skin cancer.

* A one per cent decrease in ozone could also lead to 100,000 extra blind people worldwide due to cataracts.

* Ozone depleting chemicals are estimated to be responsible for 20-25 per cent of global warming.

### Do something!

● **Avoid products made with CFCs. Never dump an old fridge, ask your local council where the CFCs can be drained.**

● **Help yourself by using a barrier suntan cream if you're going to spend a long time in the sun.**

Will the CFCs in this dumped fridge (*Above*) make the ozone hole over the antartic (*left*) even bigger? They could be safely recycled.

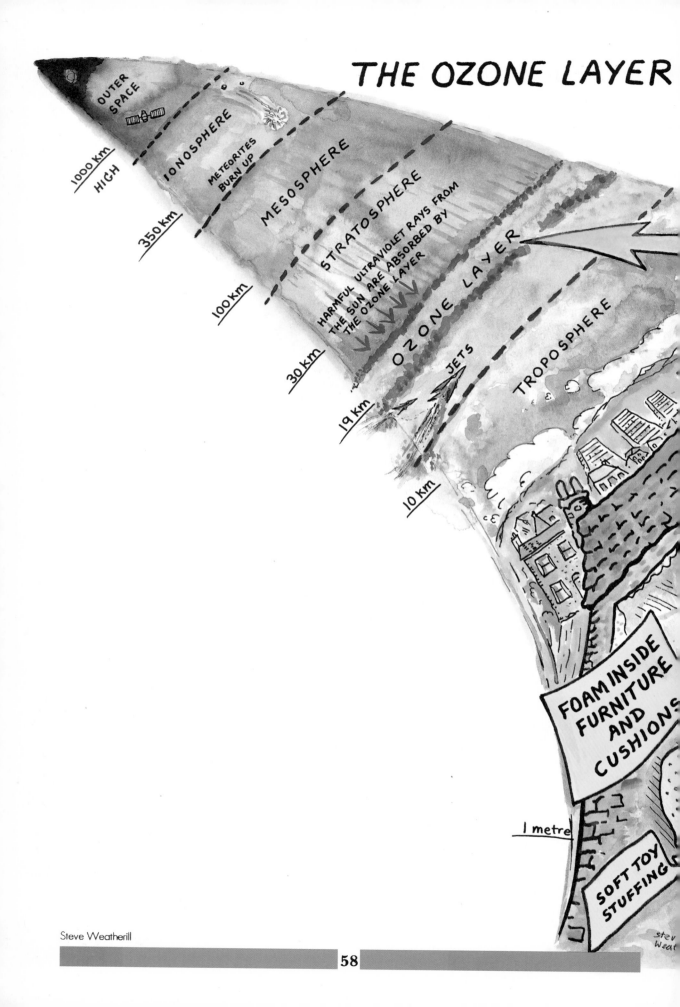

# THE OZONE LAYER

OUTER SPACE

1000 km
HIGH

350 km

IONOSPHERE

METEORITES BURN UP

MESOSPHERE

100 km

STRATOSPHERE

HARMFUL ULTRAVIOLET RAYS FROM THE SUN ARE ABSORBED BY THE OZONE LAYER

30 km

OZONE LAYER

19 km

JETS

TROPOSPHERE

10 km

FOAM INSIDE FURNITURE AND CUSHIONS

1 metre

SOFT TOY STUFFING

Steve Weatherill

Steve Weat

# HIDDEN HAZARDS IN THE HOME

# What is Friends Of The Earth?

Friends of the Earth is an organisation that works to improve the environment. We try to persuade people in government and elsewhere to protect the environment. We also let people know what is happening in the environment by producing leaflets and books such as this one.

Friends of the Earth campaign in many areas. These include the destruction of the world's tropical rainforests, water pollution, air pollution, waste and recycling, the use of energy, countryside and agriculture and transport.

## Local Groups

In Britain, Friends of the Earth have over 180,000 supporters and 280 local groups. These groups campaign, all over the country, for a better environment. Many also deal with problems that occur in just one part of the country. Some have been involved in major schemes such as 'Recycling City' in Sheffield.

Friends of the Earth International organise a world wide network of environmental groups. We have groups in over 30 countries and are active in helping local people all over the world to solve environmental problems.

Friends of the Earth have had a lot of success. We were one of the first groups to let people know about the problems of acid rain. The Friends of the Earth campaign on ozone depletion largely led to the manufacturers removing CFCs from household aerosols. We have done a lot to bring about an improvement to drinking water quality in Britain. Now the work of Friends of the Earth has become even more urgent because of major threats such as global warming.

If you are not already a member of Friends of the Earth why not join us now? You could also consider becoming a member of our youth section, Earth Action.

Now, more than ever, the Earth needs all the friends it can get.

Rachel Moreton

## Schools

Our work with young people involves helping them learn more about the environment and how to protect it. For this reason we started a brand new information service for young people and schools. We have recently produced a series of information sheets together with project ideas for children above the age of 11. If you wish to obtain these sheets or learn more about our service for young people you can do so by writing to:

*The Education Section, Friends of the Earth, 26-28 Underwood Street, London. N1 7JQ.*

# Glossary

**Acid rain**
Rain, snow, mist or hail which is made by waste gases (sulphur dioxide and nitrogen oxide) discharged into the air.

**Arable farming**
The farming of plant crops such as wheat, barley, and vegetable.

**Atmosphere**
The layer of gases that surrounds the Earth. Not counting water vapour, it consists of nitrogen (78 per cent), oxygen (21 per cent) and very tiny amounts of other gases such as carbon dioxide, neon, argon, ozone, hydrogen, krypton and others.

**Catalytic Convertor**
An extra box fitted to vehicle exhausts which converts toxic gases into harmless ones.

**Chlorofluorocarbons**
The group of chemicals which damage the ozone layer. They are found in fridges, freezers, blown-foam packaging and some aerosols.

**Conservation**
The protection of the environment, habitats and wildlife.

**Ecology**
The study of living things and their environment.

**Ecosystem**
A community of plants and animals and the environment they live in.

**Emissions**
Substances discharged into the air from factories and domestic chimneys and car exhausts.

**Environment**
The surroundings or the world that humans and all other animals and plants live in.

**Food chain**
A chain of living things which depend on each other for food. An example of a food chain is: grass grows; cows eat the grass and humans eat the cows or drink the milk.

**Global warming**
The increase in the average temperature of the Earth thought to be caused by the build-up of greenhouse gases in the atmosphere.

**Greenhouse effect**
The effect of gases such as $CO_2$ trapping the sun's heat.

**Greenhouse gases**
The name for about 30 atmospheric gases such as carbon dioxide and methane which allow the heat of the Sun to reach the Earth but trap the heat escaping back out to space.

**Ground water**
Water held in underground rocks and soil. It comes mainly from water seeping down from the surface.

**Intensive farming**
Farming which uses high levels of machinery, chemicals, fertilizer and feeds in a small area of land. Livestock kept in intensive conditions are said to be factory farmed.

**Landfill site**
A place where solid waste is disposed of, usually a hole in the ground.

**Nitrogen oxides**
Gases formed mainly from nitrogen in the atmosphere when fuels are burnt at a high temperature.

**Nutrients**
The materials which are necessary for growth and life such as water, minerals, fats, proteins and carbohydrates.

**Organic**
Any living material. A type of farming that uses no artificial chemicals.

**Ozone**
A gas similar to oxygen that forms a vital layer high up in the atmosphere, shielding the Earth from the Sun's harmful ultra-violet rays. Ozone is harmful when it occurs near the ground.

**Pesticide**
A chemical used to kill pests such as insects.

**Photosynthesis**
The process by which plants use the Sun's energy, water and carbon dioxide to form carbohydrates. Oxygen is released in the process.